Contents

FOSTERING

The Essential Guide

Diana
Cambridge

Fostering – The Essential Guide is also available in accessible formats for people with any degree of visual impairment. The large print edition and e-book (with accessibility features enabled) are available from Need2Know. Please let us know if there are any special features you require and we will do our best to accommodate your needs.

First published in Great Britain in 2012 by
Need2Know
Remus House
Coltsfoot Drive
Peterborough
PE2 9BF
Telephone 01733 898103
Fax 01733 313524
www.need2knowbooks.co.uk

Introduction

Could you be a foster parent? You've certainly picked up this book because you have an interest in the process. If you want to foster, it's an arena that has never been so welcoming – excellent fees, a carers' state pension secured, lots of training and support, plus minimal red tape.

It's a well-rewarded job calling for special applicants (though you need no qualifications or experience, other than having had contact with children) – but with plenty of opportunities.

There are so many children in care – approximately 60,000 according to the British Association for Adoption and Fostering (BAAF) – that the time between you being approved and a child being placed with you might not be very long. I fostered eight-year-old Clare for a year before adopting her, and during that time I got to know quite a few foster families and fostering social workers.

Fostering isn't a bed of roses. Your foster child could be sad and unhappy, or show challenging behaviour, or react badly with your own children. They're all problems that can be solved. There were times when I felt I hit rock bottom – but the next day was somehow always better. Social workers and others are there to help and support you: they will definitely have seen it all before!

The early days are the hardest, but as your foster child grows in confidence, you'll see a healthy, happy child starting to shine through. It may be that your child goes back to his or her birth mother, or on to adopters, or stays with you – all rewarding, all satisfying. You have a big part to play, and this will be recognised by officials.

There are excellent programmes in place to help your foster child. The Life Story Book, which every foster child has, is one of them – and you will be able to help him or her with that. Along the way, your knowledge about children's behaviour and some of the difficult backgrounds they overcome will increase.

It's a fascinating area, which can of course be disturbing – but you can look on your part in your foster child's life as one of the most valuable. Many children stay in touch with their long-term foster carers.

Knowing when a foster child's challenging behaviour stems from their difficult background, or is simply an expression of childish or teenage immaturity, is one of the big dilemmas of being a carer. The answer is – you often don't know! And it would be a mistake to constantly quiz them about their feelings. Sometimes you have to act by instinct, and sometimes – as I often did – you get it wrong.

That's where this handbook can help. As a former foster parent, I think I've been through most of the trials and fallen into plenty of the pitfalls . . . I've learned so much.

This handbook covers all the stages of fostering, with plenty of practical tips and advice. At the end of a bad day, it's there for you to confirm that you're not the only one who finds fostering gruelling one day and joyful the next. It will reassure you that you are doing the right thing – and that sometimes there is no right thing.

What's great is that you're giving a child the most generous gift of a home, love and friendship. Most of all you offer your time. You've changed things for them, and made a successful future a real possibility. Most foster parents think fostering is the best thing they've ever done . . . and perhaps you too will be encouraged to go ahead.

Step by step, this emotive and informative guide will be with you all the way.

Chapter One

First Thoughts on Fostering

You're thinking about fostering – one of the most rewarding jobs you can have today. Approximately 59,000 children live with foster families in the United Kingdom. During 2012, fostering services were looking for at least 8,750 new foster families to offer safe and secure homes to children who need them.

A real job

Could you be one of these foster carers?

Gone are the days when fostering was looked at as something done out of kindness by little old ladies living in Hansel and Gretel cottages. That was the stereotype. Fostering now is a professional job, with good earnings – £400-£500 plus a week for some placements – and it counts towards your pension.

You don't have to pay tax on the first £10,000 of your fostering earnings. There's ongoing training (both online and at local workshops and courses), special allowances for birthdays, Christmas and holidays, and support . . . someone to talk to whenever you have problems.

One of the big plus factors of fostering is that you can earn while being home-based. If you foster school-aged children, the day is your own, for relaxation or enjoying your hobbies . . . and knowing you have a pay cheque coming in every week or month. Of course, there will be meetings and other events to attend, but the work is much more flexible than an office or shop job.

'Fostering now is a professional job, with good earnings – £400-£500 plus a week for some placements – and it counts towards your pension.'

Not just the money!

But as good as the financial rewards are, money isn't the main reason people foster. All of us look for job satisfaction, for employment that's emotionally rewarding, varied and fits in with our interests.

I have an adopted daughter and, though I have never been a long-term foster parent, like all adoptive parents we had to foster Clare for a year 'with a view to adoption.'

We got to know her foster family and other foster carers, which gave me a taste of just how interesting (but also at times demanding) fostering could be.

'There couldn't be a more generous thing to do.'

Older children need help too

You can foster children of all ages – from babies to teenagers. If you have the room, you can foster siblings. There is no shortage of children waiting to be looked after.

About twenty percent of children in care are 16 or older, and these are the children that can really benefit from being looked after and mentored. Your help will give them a great introduction to working life.

If you foster a series of children, there's no reason why you shouldn't keep in touch with them for years. Once they are adults, they may want to visit you – to them you've been a mum and the home you offered was theirs.

There couldn't be a more generous thing to do.

Key role

Clare's foster family had had several children in their care. They lived in the country, with a pony and pets, and did marvellous work with their children. I remember the foster mother enjoyed cooking and what she dished up was always delicious.

They looked after Clare – who came from a background of serious neglect – for more than two years, seeing her through ups and downs – meetings with her birth mother and the pain and sadness of the final separation and goodbye – and then prepared her to be adopted.

8

It was a lot of trauma for a child of eight, and much work, too, for the foster parents, which they did with great love and selflessness.

Foster carers such as Clare's play a key role in transforming children's lives.

Why do foster carers look after children?

Children need fostering because:

▨ It gives their own families a chance to sort out their problems, which can include depression, drug or alcohol abuse, and illness.

▨ Many have been the victims of abuse or neglect.

▨ Their own mother or both parents may have died.

As a foster carer, you can also look after:

▨ Young mothers and babies.

▨ Young mothers with toddlers or older children.

▨ Teenagers needing very short-term accommodation and support.

The legals

Foster children continue to be legally part of their own family, even if there is limited contact with them. It is not the same as adoption, which provides a 'forever family' for a child and which ends their legal relationship with their birth family. At 18 they are free to contact their birth family if they wish to.

But whatever the legalities, children in long-term foster care, which could last for the whole of their childhood, will likely see the foster mother as 'Mum'.

'Whatever the legalities, children in long-term foster care, which could last for the whole of their childhood, will likely see the foster mother as "Mum".'

Children do well

Children who are successfully fostered long term will probably do better in life than those who are moved around to a series of families, plus moved back to and from their birth parents.

Children who have been in successful foster care:

- Are more likely to go to college and university.

- Come to terms more easily with the traumas of their early life.

- Have more chance to make healthy relationships of their own in later life.

Foster stars

Marilyn Monroe was one of the world's most famous foster children. Brought up in a series of foster homes, adorable yet vulnerable, she died much too soon. If she'd been alive now, the help she'd have had in coming to terms with her early years might have saved her – who knows?

Other famous foster children include: Babe Ruth, James Dean, Bruce Oldfield and Eleanor Roosevelt, the wife of the 32nd president of the USA.

And, of course, Harry Potter and Superman are both fostered children!

Who's eligible?

Who can be a foster carer?

The good news is: almost anyone can apply.

- You have to be 18 (some agencies prefer 21) but there's no upper age limit.

- You don't have to be married – you can be single, living with someone or on your own.

- You can be gay and living with a gay partner.

- Foster carers come from diverse ethnic and cultural backgrounds.

- You don't have to own your own home, but if you live in rented accommodation you would need the landlord's approval.

- You don't have to have been to college, or have any special qualifications.

- You don't have to have had your own children, but experience of caring for children will be helpful.

People with convictions for sexual or violent offences against children are not eligible.

What do foster carers do?

They provide children with day-to-day care, just as they do for their own children – and much more. You are opening your home to a child who might have had traumatic experiences, and it's part of your job to help them come to terms with this.

As foster carer you support the child in his or her education, look after their health and promote their social wellbeing. It means the child, thanks to you, is exposed to normal, healthy family life and sharing in events such as family Christmases and birthdays, plus sports, pets, games and outings. The best foster carers offer their foster children exactly what they provide for their own children.

But because they are foster children, with inevitably challenging backgrounds, the role will not be quite as straightforward as bringing up your own children. When it goes well, nothing can be more rewarding than to see a formerly distressed and sad child begin to flourish. But you do need patience!

Meetings

You need to be reasonably well organised; the role includes attending meetings, keeping records, buying everything your child needs, visiting his or her school, keeping photos and scrapbooks for your foster child and arranging contact with birth families. It helps to keep a diary, and be a list-maker! But you don't have to provide invoices and receipts for everything you spend.

You will receive a great deal of pre- and post-approval training and support to help you develop the skills for the job. There are courses and workshops, books and online training – there's no shortage of professional development, but at the same time the role doesn't carry the stress of an office or corporate job.

'When it goes well, nothing can be more rewarding than to see a formerly distressed and sad child begin to flourish. But you do need patience!'

Big decision

Deciding to foster a child is a big step. The first rung of the ladder is making an application, and then being assessed. Naturally, you will be apprehensive about what an assessment entails. To take the first step, contact your local council's fostering team in the family services department.

Also look online under 'fostering' – there are many independent agencies as well, all competing for your services. All independent fostering agencies (as well as local authority ones) are regulated and must meet government standards. The government recommends you look at what several agencies – both local authority and independent – have to offer (you should be able to see their Ofsted ratings) before you make a final choice.

But with every agency, you must go through the assessment, training and then the approval process. The standards are robust with all agencies: all foster careers must meet these.

Take heart – it's not as bad as you think!

'The standards are robust with all agencies: all foster careers must meet these.'

Summing Up

- During 2012, fostering services were looking for at least 8,750 new foster families to offer safe and secure homes to children who need them.

- One of the big plus factors of fostering is that you can earn while being home-based.

- You can foster children of all ages – from babies to teenagers. If you have the room, you can foster siblings. There is no shortage of children waiting to be looked after.

- Job satisfaction and flexibility – not money – are the main reasons people foster, although the financial incentives are good.

- Almost anyone can apply to foster. You have to be 18 – some agencies prefer 21 – but there's no upper age limit. You don't have to be married; you can be single, living with someone, or on your own. You can be gay and living with a gay partner – foster carers come from a diverse range of ethnic and cultural backgrounds.

- You need to be reasonably well organised: there is paperwork.

- You will receive a great deal of pre- and post-approval training and support to help you develop the skills for the job.

Chapter Two

Have You Got
What it Takes?

Before you make your official application, ask yourself this: Have I got what it takes to be a foster carer?

You don't need professional qualifications – or any qualification – but there are basic character skills which you need. Here's a checklist:

Are you a good listener?

Sometimes we think we have to give advice when we listen, that we have to respond. Yet it's often when we don't give advice, or respond, that our listening is at its most acute.

Children don't always find it easy to talk, and they might think they'll be told off for doing things, or even thinking about them. A foster child might feel reluctant to tell you, for example, how lonely they are in the foster home, how they miss their mother. This is when you can really help, with empathy rather than sympathy.

Admit your real feelings

It was only when I told Clare I hated my mother when I was a toddler and that I wanted to kill her, that Clare – who'd just said she hated me – looked impressed.

Once, after she'd raged and cried, I said: 'I know inside you there's a small, frightened Clare – I understand that.' Again, she responded.

'You don't need professional qualifications – or any qualification – but there are basic character skills which you need.'

This was so much better than what I'd been doing before, trying to 'reform' her or 'make her behave' or getting involved in arguments with her. There's more on this in later chapters.

Listen well

I don't think I really listened to anyone properly until I took a private therapy certificate course, which included listening skills. The longer you can 'hold the silence' but with a kind presence, the better this will be. You can defuse anger and help to tease out worries.

Say less, but provide more comfort.

Are you an organiser?

'Say less, but provide more comfort.'

If you are fostering more than one child – and perhaps have your own – there's a fair amount of logistics to be handled here. You'll need to keep to careful track of meetings, health appointments, school events, contact visits, dentists, hobbies and sports dates . . . plus you need to organise some time for yourself.

You can organise it all on a computer, though I still prefer old-fashioned diaries! The one thing I wish I'd done is keep an up-to-date record of social workers' contact details, and other people involved in Clare's early days. You don't need sophisticated organisation abilities, but you need to stay on top of the essential admin. Make it pleasant – attractive diary and notebook, neat desk top, pot of plenty of pens and scratch pad for messages. Colourful pin board – pin up those essential tickets, receipts, instruction booklets, notices from school and other essential stuff instantly

Are you confident?

There will probably be difficult situations to handle – perhaps not with your child, but in dealing with birth parents or with potential adoptive parents. Birth mothers might be critical of you and their behaviour may be very different to yours – you could feel overwhelmed and offended. Yet inside, they might be finding your home intimidating.

16

This is when you'll need confidence. You need to be polite but firm, and be able to ignore provocative remarks or behaviour. Not all birth families will be like this! There will be those you can get on with easily. The trick is to treat them all with fairness, and try not to take anything personally.

If you've ever worked in a call centre, in customer service, teaching, nursing, retail or many other people-facing jobs, you'll be confident in your ability to handle tricky situations. Always defuse. Don't be defensive, try to help.

Are you fair?

Treating all of the children in your house fairly comes as second nature to most mums. It's just more so with the foster child – they shouldn't feel like a second-class citizen. At the same time, neither should your own children; it's just as easy for them to feel ignored while all the attention is on the foster child.

That said, there are numerous reports of birth children taking great pleasure in welcoming foster children, enjoying having them around, and making good friends with them. If you do have your own children it can be a great asset in settling the foster child in.

Equal gifts

If you bring sweets or some other small gift home for your own child, bring something for the foster child, too. It's not the value, but the warmth of the gesture.

At Christmas, make it plain you'd love them to join in with you – but be prepared for possible moodiness and the child wanting to be alone. This is not uncommon with foster children at Christmas and other celebrations.

Are you patient?

This is one quality I was most short of when we first had Clare. The thing about children in care is that they will often not let an argument drop; they will keep on and on. Their anger doesn't seem to reach a natural peak then fall away; it just stays at the peak.

Don't punish – withhold privileges

You do get training in how to ignore it and walk away, resisting the temptation to respond – and that's the best thing to do . . . don't get involved. At the same time, I don't think you should punish the child for what he or she says. Bad behaviour – what they do rather than what they say – is another matter. The best response to that might be to withhold privileges such as going out with friends or watching TV.

When things have simmered down, don't bear a grudge. Don't resent what's said as a result of the hard time this child has had. Their feelings will get the better of them from time to time.

For you, make time for a 'tranquillising' class such as yoga, Zumba, salsa, swimming or whatever nourishing activities you really enjoy.

Is your home stable?

'Your home should be welcoming and safe.'

Your home should be welcoming and safe. Children should be able to feel that this is a real home; that parents won't be moody or unpredictable, and that meals and clean clothes will arrive regularly. The first welcome is important – this is when children are at their most anxious, confused and sad, and very possibly angry. They didn't ask to be moved into a stranger's house. They don't deserve the pain they've had.

Are you perceptive?

The ability to reflect is valued by social workers looking for carers. Often what happens on the surface – what a child says or how they behave – doesn't really represent what goes on in their mind. Can you get beneath the exterior behaviour? Can you make allowances? To do this, you don't have to probe and question. It's best just to listen and reflect. There are lots of good books on 'attachment disorder', which most foster children suffer from. This wasn't mentioned much when we had Clare – it's now considered important. Knowing more at that time would have explained a lot to me.

Are you energetic?

It's another vital quality. You'd be amazed just how much energy foster children use – of yours! They are demanding. If they begin to flourish, they may want to show off new skills and talents all the time. If you have the energy to join in with them and spend time watching and praising . . . all to the good. Sometimes it's worth dropping the chores just to enjoy your foster child.

My tried and tested checklist

Here's my own checklist of abilities it's helpful to have, based on my experience.

Humour

Foster parents shouldn't be strict, rigid or too serious – that won't help with children. If you can see the funny side of life, that's a definite asset! Also, watch as many comedies as you can on DVD . . . the more you can laugh the better.

Optimism

When things look at their worst – and there were often occasions like that with Clare – you need to visualise the future as being successful. Fast-forward a few years and see the foster child as happy boy or girl, reaching their own potential. Hang on to that.

Flexibility

Things can change suddenly. Perhaps the plans for the child have to be altered, meetings or appointments are rescheduled or cancelled, the child's birth family circumstances change, social workers might be ill or have to attend urgent meetings, your child might have a change of mind about the plans you've made. The more flexible you can be the better. Fostering is inevitably a work in progress – there can be no certainties.

Forward-looking

It's a great help if you can see the long-term picture. If you foster a child who is being adopted, and you've grown attached to him or her, it's hard not to cherish the rapport you've established. Yet the adoptive parents are making a long-term commitment – a lifetime one.

Enjoy cooking

One thing I loved was making food, baking kids' cakes (which I've never done again since Clare was small) and entertaining other children. Making up party bags and wrapping small, inexpensive prizes for games was a delight. If you love to cook, you'll enjoying dishing up something tasty every evening; but if you really do dislike cooking and homemaking, then fostering will seem a bit of a chore.

'The more flexible you can be the better. Fostering is inevitably a work in progress – there can be no certainties.'

Basic tips on catering

You should be able to get cash 'n' carry card – usually by showing that you are self-employed, which all foster carers are. The card might not be helpful for all of your shopping, but items that could be bought in bulk cheaply include:

- Loo rolls.
- Soap powder.
- Bars of soap.
- Toothpastes.
- Cooking oil.
- Pasta sauces.
- Big jars of coffee.
- Tea.
- Frozen goods such as pizza and chips.

A book I can recommend for really economical cooking is *The New Pauper's Cookbook* by Jocasta Innes (get a cheap copy on Amazon).

Cost it!

If you really want to challenge yourself on catering cheaply, then cost everything, and work out how many meals you can get from one major buy – for example a large fresh chicken. It might seem expensive to start with, but by the time you've had hot roast chicken, cold roast chicken, chicken sandwiches, chicken soup and maybe a stir fry, your chicken has gone a very long way. Perhaps too long! But to this day, Clare says her favourite meal is roast chicken with roast potatoes and Yorkshire puddings. But, kids also love pizza, fish fingers, burgers and pasta, and ethnic food – Thai, Indian, Chinese. Waitrose is surprisingly economical for ethnic and delicious ready meals.

Packed lunch

For packed lunches, a good sandwich, crisps, drink and a piece of fruit should be enough. Sandwiches can be filled with tuna or chicken, a little mayonnaise and a bit of lettuce in wholemeal bread. Most children will eat these.

Clean up!

I am not the world's best housekeeper, as anyone who knows me will confirm; I can be very untidy, and I lose things. But I do enjoy making order out of chaos. I love it when the house looks nice.

If there are regular meetings at your house, you need it to look tidy and welcoming.

Professional clean – at no cost

Take a few tips from a cleaner friend of mine. This is his advice for a daily clean that can be done and dusted in 30 minutes:

1. Work from the top to the bottom of the house.

2. Start by spraying limescale remover on taps and loo.

3. Spray normal cleaner on bath and kitchen surfaces. Leave.

4. Empty waste bins and old newspapers etc. into bin bags.

5. Keep a large wicker basket in each room and throw clutter into it.

6. Put laundry into washer. Switch on.

7. Put dishes etc. into the sink or dishwasher – switch on.

8. Make beds, tidy clothes.

9. Sponge and wipe off all the cleaners in the kitchen and bathroom. Give the loo an extra spray and clean, inside and out.

10. Put jars etc. into kitchen cupboards, leaving kitchen surfaces uncluttered and clean.

11. Very rapid sponge of kitchen/bathroom floors.

'If there are regular meetings at your house, you need it to look tidy and welcoming.'

Top tips:

- When you've washed and wiped surfaces, dry them with kitchen paper towel. You'll have a hotel-calibre gleam.

- A handful of flowers – from your garden or a local market – enhance the welcome of your living room . . . even if you only do this for meetings!

Less means more

- Leave polishing and vacuum cleaning to one morning a week.

- Iron as little as possible. I have friends who never iron – and their kids look fine.

- Buy school clothes from chain stores – you don't need to iron them, just hang.

- Buy cheap socks in sets of six all the same colour. (Try Primark, the cheapest and best store for almost any clothes.)

Speak up!

As a foster mum or dad, you're also an advocate for the foster child – someone who can speak up for them. As you get to know them better, you'll become aware of their frailties, their insecurities, doubts and fears.

At the regular meetings you attend, there will be social workers and other professionals, but you will most probably be the one who knows this child best – especially if they've lived with you for some time.

You're the one

It's you who sees them when they're happy, in despair and angry. You might have been involved in tiring scenes, and had to put up with seriously bad behaviour.

You see him or her at their least appealing and not just during working hours from 9 to 5. You can't say goodbye and go back to your own life, in the way that social workers – despite all the excellent work they do – are able to. You have to live with this child, and your observations and insights will count.

Strengthen bonds

Strengthening the bond with a new foster child can be done in simple, practical ways.

You could try:

- Pinboards with pictures and mementoes for each child.

- A blackboard on which they can write messages.

- Magnetic shopping lists on the fridge – write down what you're running out of, and encourage foster children to do the same.

- A patch of the garden for the foster child to grow their own choice of flowers or veg.

- If you have pets, give the child a small, easy task in its care.

'As a foster mum or dad, you're also an advocate for the foster child – someone who can speak up for them.'

Summing Up

- Listening skills are vital.
- Patience and fairness are musts.
- You'll need energy and optimism.
- It's a plus if you enjoy cooking.
- Make your home welcoming.
- You are the one who speaks up for the foster child.
- Offer him or her a mini-garden and space on the family pinboard.
- Your views on the foster child's progress count.

Chapter Three

You Pass Assessment!

You believe you have what it takes and you're looking forward to applying for the job of foster carer. It's a self-employed position and your fee can be paid straight into your bank account.

Being home-based does not mean you'll lose out on your state pension – fostering is seen as a 'proper' job now, not just a 'staying at home caring for children' occupation, as it used to be. You'll get training, workshops and continued professional development. But first you have to pass your assessment – and then be approved for a specific placement.

Before you even apply, read as much as you can about fostering today. There are so many agencies, so many specialities, so many ways of fostering.

'There's been a real shift over the past 15 years or so in how fostering is seen,' says Sarah Acheson of Bath & NE Somerset's children's service. 'There are so many fostering agencies competing for the best people who want to foster. It's regarded as a definite job, self-employed but with pension rights protected.'

> 'Many foster carers think courses add extra interest to the job and make it more professional, though the core requirement is caring for the children.'

Perks and benefits

What are the plus and minus points? It's a job that gives you some professional development and a choice of extra training to keep you updated. There are workshops which get you out of the house . . . and give you a reason to get a bit dressed up now and then!

You can meet social workers and other foster carers, or add certificates and qualifications to your CV. Many foster carers think courses add extra interest to the job and make it more professional, though the core requirement is caring for the children.

Plus points

Fees for fostering are good (from around £200 to £500 plus per week, per child, plus allowances) and if children in care have special talents – in sports, drama, music etc. – there is state money which foster carers can draw on to pay for extra fees and kit. Pocket money, school meals, holiday packed lunch allowance, school uniform and equipment are all met by the state.

The foster carer meets no expenses from their own pocket (though some generous foster carers choose to, perhaps including foster children in family treats and holidays abroad), and invoices and receipts don't usually have to be provided.

Where meals are concerned, you treat the foster child as you would your own child – so you control your own budgeting and housekeeping any way you like. You don't have to show your food bills or housekeeping bills or laundry/clothes bills – look after your foster child as if they're one of yours: they're not a separate 'expense'. Where anything can be shared, share it!

'The job can be exhausting and sometimes seem thankless. Perhaps that's true for all jobs, not just fostering!'

Profit

Your fostering fee should enable you to earn a reasonable 'profit' – as in any job. In all employment, we might have some job expenses – office clothes, travel, snacks and drinks – but we also expect to have earnings that make the job worthwhile financially.

Minus points

As a foster carer, your 'office expenses' would be minimal, as you're working from home. But that's also a price you pay – opening your home to extra children, with inconvenience and challenges as well as rewards and pleasures – and you deserve to make some earnings from that. The challenges can be seen as a minus point: the job can be exhausting and sometimes seem thankless. Perhaps that's true for all jobs, not just fostering!

Options

You need to think first about what type of fostering you want to do. You can specialise if you prefer, and are approved for that. There are different options for fostering:

- Providing emergency or short-term care for youngsters who might have been in trouble.

- Giving accommodation and a friendly ear for mothers and babies (or toddlers).

- Offering a permanent childhood home to a boy or girl until they reach adulthood.

- Caring temporarily for children who will be returned to their own families.

- Looking after children who will be prepared for adoption. (There's more on adoption preparation in a later chapter.)

'All fosters carers can mentor with advice and life skills for children from age 4 to 18 – it's part of the job,' says social worker Sarah Acheson. 'There is plenty of support for foster carers, and an obligation to continue with training.'

Which placement?

You'll need to decide what kind of placements you'd like to be considered for.

- Only long-term placements?

- Care for children whose plan could include preparation for adoption?

- Would you prefer babies or small children?

- Short-term or emergency placements?

- Would you like to look after disabled children or those with challenging behaviour?

Foster carers are approved for specific numbers, age ranges and genders and also for either long-term (permanent) or short-term (temporary) places. A carer might, for example, be approved for one long-term placement of a specific child and another short-term placement.

You know best

Whatever you decide, social workers will try to meet your requirements – only you know best what you can and can't manage.

'Foster carers are approved for specific numbers, age ranges and genders and also for either long-term (permanent) or short-term (temporary) places.'

A carer who wants to offer only long-term places would not have a child placed on a short-term basis. When 'short-term' children are placed, social workers usually do not know at that stage what the long-term plan will be.

The law, and good practice, requires that the child should return to parents or extended family members if and when that is safely possible. If that does not happen, and there's a plan for adoption or long-term fostering, the task of the short-term carer is to support that process as the child moves to the new family.

Long-term fostering

In some circumstances, the carers might want to be assessed to become long-term foster carers or even adopters for that child.

Mentor and mend

Some young people have regular mentoring sessions with their foster carer as part of their placement. There are a number of schemes, including some which are specifically for young people on the edge of, or already involved in, offending.

These placements will probably be challenging, but if they work well, the rewards are huge. You will have helped to change a young person's life and possibly set them on the road to success, after years of difficulty.

Tools of the trade

You are applying for a job, and there are some similarities with conventional job application. You are interviewed (though not in a formal way – this will be at your own home) and assessed, you need to give the names of people who will provide references for you, and you will have to show that you have the qualities needed for the job.

Your tools of the trade are a suitable room for the child, a stable household – and you!

Personality plus

Perhaps more than with most other jobs, landing this one requires the right personality. The foster parent's responsibility is to care for the child as if he or she were a member of the family. Plans and encouragement for their future must also be given in the same spirit that you'd show to help your own child.

No job shortage

All the qualities you need are outlined in the previous chapter, and if you can offer most of these you're already on the long list! What's on your side is that unlike most areas of employment these days, there is a shortage of applicants – the number of jobs available is much greater than the than the number of qualified applicants. Sadly, that's unlikely to change – children in care always need foster parents.

Most local council-run children's homes closed at least 15 years ago. Now, family homes are considered a much better environment for a child to grow up in.

However, it's assessment – as to whether you are suitable for the job and then approval for a named child – that counts.

'The foster parent's responsibility is to care for the child as if he or she were a member of the family.'

How to start

You've thought about it – so now you need to look on the Internet or in the phone book to find local fostering services, including the one run by your own district or county council. Many advertise in local newspapers and magazines.

Choice of agencies

Choose a fostering service, get in touch with them and ask for an information pack.

Read it thoroughly, and then indicate your interest by phone, letter or email. You will be invited to attend an information session and meet foster carers and social workers. It's a friendly and informative evening.

Apply now!

If you feel comfortable with everything so far – and think this could possibly be a job for you – make a formal application, usually by letter. All of the details that you need to give will have been included in your information pack, or given out at the introductory info session.

'Social workers are not looking for "posh homes" or carers with any specific childcare background.'

Social worker support

Once your application has been received and it's clear you satisfy all of the basics, the assessment begins. A social worker supports you through this process. They carry out an assessment of you, your household and your background – though this is always friendly. Social workers are not looking for 'posh homes' or carers with any specific childcare background.

Visits

He or she will make several visits to your home – at your convenience – and you'll discuss what you can offer foster children and what kind of fostering you'd prefer to do. They will talk a bit about your own background and upbringing.

Need2Know

There's nothing to be frightened of. It's not like a formal job interview. Social workers aren't looking for ways to exclude you. They always have more vacancies to fill than applicants to fill them. At the same time, standards are high. It's important that only the people with the right qualities are accepted for the work.

Must-do training

While you are being assessed, there is obligatory training, which prepares you and your household for fostering. You learn why children are in care, what kind of care plans can be made for them, and something about the legal system.

There's advice and practical tips on fostering from experienced carers. There's no exam to be taken. It's all very relaxed and informal, as well as being professional. Usually it's training that won't cut into your current work time – an evening a week or fortnight for a few weeks.

Training, workshops, Open University courses

Once you become a foster carer, you can keep on learning and enhancing your CV, which is useful not only for fostering but also for any other work you choose to do in the future.

There's free training and workshops. There are also optional courses through the Open University, ideal for foster carers, or potential carers. No academic qualifications are needed for the OU, and you don't have to do a whole degree; you can do just a social care course, and get credits and certificates for it. There are courses in helping young children to progress, with lively networks and forums set up by foster carers. OU courses are not free, but you can get discounts and bursaries. Log on to http://www.open.ac.uk/contact for more details.

Assessed then approved

Foster carers are assessed as suitable to foster, and then approved for a specific child or children – as we've said, the two processes are separate. But there needn't be a huge time gap between the two. Fostering agencies and the government are keen to speed up the process and cut the red tape to an essential minimum.

Checks

As part of your assessment, social workers make background checks on you. They have to be absolutely confident that children will be safe and well cared for, so there are police checks, a health check from your GP, and interviews with your two referees.

'Exciting times are ahead! Celebrate your success.'

When the assessment and all the paperwork is done – allow five months at least – your application goes to a meeting of the fostering panel, which comprises of magistrates, GPs and other professionals. You don't attend this meeting.

The panel recommends you as suitable to foster, but it's the fostering service that makes the final decision. In practice, once you've been approved by the fostering panel, it's highly unlikely that your fostering agency would decide not to use you.

So, you've been satisfactorily assessed and approved: a child will now be matched with your family. It could be within the next few weeks – or even the next day. Exciting times are ahead! Celebrate your success.

Summing Up

- The job is self-employed.

- Your state pension is protected even though you're home-based.

- Begin by choosing a foster agency.

- Attend an introduction information evening.

- You do pre-approval training during assessment.

- Social workers are not looking for 'posh homes' or carers with any specific childcare background.

- There is ongoing training and workshops.

- You can choose to take Open University courses useful for foster carers.

- Checks are made on you – health, police and referees.

- You decide what type of placement you can manage.

- You may be matched with a child quickly after approval.

Chapter Four

Matched!

You're matched! Your first foster child is on their way to you. It's an exciting but nervous time. You don't know what to expect.

If you have other children, you will have prepared them for the new arrival.

Maybe they can have a tiny offering to give – a few sweets, a soft toy, a game – nothing costly.

It's their time that will be the most precious, and the cheerfulness of their greeting. Having your own boy or girl show the foster child round your home is invaluable – but if you don't have children, then your own warmth and attention is fine.

Settling in

How should you settle in a new child?

These are five top tips from an experienced foster carer, Carey Meredith, who lives near Bristol. She has fostered many children over the years. She has her own daughter but usually has one or two fosters: one has been with her for seven years and will stay until he moves into his own accommodation.

1. Foster children always remember the first meal they had at your house. Make it tasty. Carey always serves spaghetti Bolognese – almost all kids like it!

2. 'When the child arrives, there must be no probing, no questions. The child is bewildered enough and possibly angry already – to be subjected to questions would be the last straw,' says Carey. Your welcome should be low-key, yet they should be in no doubt that you're glad to see them.

3. Don't list 'house rules' the moment they check in.

4. If you have other children, let them show the newbie around.

> 'Having your own boy or girl show the foster child round your home is invaluable – but if you don't have children, then your own warmth and attention is fine.'

5. Any pets? Most children love to stroke pets – these can be a great asset in settling in little ones.

Nerves

You might know a lot about the child who is coming to you, or you may have received an emergency phone call just two hours before. If you know quite a bit about them, you might even have met their parents.

The prospect of caring for someone else's child is a huge responsibility, but remember that the foster child will be much more fearful than you are.

On that first day, you should go out of your way to make the child welcome, but without giving too much oppressive attention. Gentleness works better than overenthusiasm.

'Early days are the time when they most need your help and support.'

First, names

What to call you? It's up to them – they might call you Mum and Dad, or by your first names. Let them decide, but offer the choice.

House rules

You need the foster child to fit in with the way you run your house.

The family the young person comes from might have had very different house rules from your own – or no house rules at all – but the first day isn't the day to outline your expectations.

These can come gradually. Early days are the time when they most need your help and support. If, for example, you expect each child in the family to tidy their room, this might be something the foster child has never done. For a little while you can offer to help them tidy their room, to show them how it's done.

Show them how

There may be many 'ordinary' tasks and chores – such as clearing the table after a meal – that your foster child has no experience of, so it is important to show them.

I can remember when Clare, our daughter, first arrived as a foster child with a view to adoption. She saw me lighting a fire and suggested that we just throw handfuls of lit matches on the fire to ignite it – this was what she had seen at home. She was eight then.

Yet because she had been fostered before coming to us, she also had some very good habits that had been conveyed to her by her previous foster family – she'd been with them two years.

These are worth passing on to your own foster child:

- Write down simple lists of items to remember, for example, things to take on weekends away and to take back home again. List-making is a wonderful habit for a child to pick up!
- Keep toiletries in a bag – toothbrush etc. – plus any medicines the child needs to use.
- Put clothes for washing in a carrier bag.
- Keep lists of phone numbers, addresses etc. on a special sheet of paper in their bag – remember, foster children may be moving between households. They may go back and forth to birth family or respite care.

No questions please

I felt I questioned Clare too much when she first arrived, constantly asking her how she was feeling and so on. Much better to help the child relax with food they'll enjoy and a DVD.

We took her out and about in Bath, showing her all the tourist sights – this was really too much for a little girl. I know she enjoyed some of it, but the experiences she genuinely enjoyed were:

- Going to the cinema to see kids' films.

- Spending time at the pets' department in a garden centre.
- Visiting fairgrounds or the seaside.
- Having ice creams out.

. . . all simple pleasures.

Find friends

I don't think it was until she made friends who'd come and play after school that she felt really comfortable.

She did enjoy planting things in the garden – she had her own patch – and baking cakes . . . but not always – moods were variable!

She loved being read to – and I made up stories which turned into serials, usually featuring mermaid princesses and baby bears.

School

'When it comes to school life and activities, foster children should feel they are in the same position as children who are not in care.'

The aim is to keep children in their own area whenever possible, so they should not have to keep changing schools. But if the child does have to go to a new school, meet the head teacher first and tell him or her about the child's background.

Don't be surprised if this doesn't always get passed on as they progress through school – so that some teachers won't know they are fostered. I'm not sure if this is a good or bad thing. Being in care might account for some of the problems they might experience at school, but then again it might not be!

The main thing, I think, is that when it comes to school life and activities, foster children should feel they are in the same position as children who are not in care. Encourage them to invite new friends to tea, to hold small parties and to go to them, choose presents for friends, go on school trips and join school clubs.

Pocket money

Social workers might suggest an 'official' sum to be given as pocket money. In Carey's case, the proposed weekly figure was larger than the amount she gave to her own daughter. She decided to stick to her own amount, and give both children the same – a wise move, in my view. You can make your own decisions on these matters.

Routine rules

A family routine is an absolute must. The foster child must have a taste of an orderly, pleasant family life. Household routines, such as mealtimes, need to be predictable: things should run smoothly, though not oppressively so – as in all families, there's bound to be the occasional domestic crisis!

For the new arrival, this might be the first time they have experienced what it's like to live without chaos. Regular meals, a clean and comfortable house, a cosy bedroom, people who talk normally rather than shout – all this may be new to them.

Timely tea

Carey always serves tea at 5.15pm – it's a routine. But your foster child might not be used to sitting at a table – it's possible that meals were a succession of fast foods served up in paper bags washed down with tins of soft drinks, or that meals were unpredictable at best.

Here's where you start as you mean to go on, but expect the new child to be perhaps quiet, or even sullen.

Carey's routine is for each member of the family to talk in turn about the day they've had, over tea – an excellent way to help children make simple conversation, interact with others and not just munch silently. Carey calls this 'doing our days'. But it's unlikely your new child will be able to join in this to start with, so do not expect them to.

Some help

Carey's children help to clear the table, but she doesn't expect much in the way of kitchen or household chores. She feels that would be unrealistic for any child. Helping out shouldn't be an oppressive responsibility.

She limits the amount of time they watch TV and play on computers. A set bedtime is an absolute.

Sit a little

When she thinks the time is right, Carey will sit on the floor or the child's bed, and explain that she is there to look after them. Sometimes they imagine a foster mum is there to punish them. She stresses that she is on their side.

You should offer to sit with the child at bedtime, stay with them as they go to sleep – if that's what they want. At first, some children want to be alone.

If you already have other children in your house – your own or other foster kids – it could be them who sit with the new child and help he or she settle in, or read a story. Introduce things gently.

Don't make it better

If the child cries or is very upset, don't try to 'make it better'. Harsh as it seems, it can be good for a child to cry. Just being there is enough to help them.

Often a child will have been removed from his or her own parents, usually as an emergency, because of neglect or harm. It might be that they have suffered bereavement or parental illness.

All these experiences are traumatic, so expect some challenging behaviour.

Thanks, but no thanks

Do not expect him or her to be grateful to you for taking them into your home, or even to like you.

Joining your household isn't what they expected from life. They didn't ask to have such an unhappy childhood, nor did they deserve it.

So, no matter what little treats or comforts you have ready or how much you go out of your way to welcome them, don't expect automatic thanks or recognition for your efforts.

May like, may not

Carey says that some foster children haven't liked her and, try as she might, she hasn't liked them very much. It's not something foster parents should feel guilty about. You are offering your own home to a child who needs one – and even if there is lack of rapport, you will still care, feed and protect them, and try to give them a taste of normal family life. Their own might be in chaos. They might be feeling a lot of pain.

You are doing an impressive job – one that many people couldn't even begin to attempt. So give yourself a pat on the back!

'No matter what little treats or comforts you have ready or how much you go out of your way to welcome them, don't expect automatic thanks or recognition for your efforts.'

Summing Up

- Make the first meal a tasty one – foster children always remember the first meal at your house.

- Don't probe or ask questions.

- Sit with the child at bedtime, if that is what they want.

- Other children are excellent at settling a new child in.

- Pets provide a great welcome.

- Remember that the foster child might be upset and angry.

- Don't feel guilty if you don't like the child. Still offer warmth and care.

- You are doing a great job that few could do!

Chapter Five

Life Story

The Life Story Book

There's a precious scrapbook which is part of every foster child's luggage – the Life Story Book. Maintaining it is important, and interesting, work for the foster carer.

If you are fostering for the first time, the Life Story Book – which every child in care has and which they carry with them to each placement – might come as a surprise to you, even a shock. It is a record of their past and present, and it might help to shape their future.

Memory bank

The books come in a variety of forms: photograph albums, scrapbooks, written accounts and perhaps audio and video recordings. They might include drawings, poems, family trees, letters, bus and train tickets and all sorts of ephemera that evoke the past, record individual histories and provide clues to identity. It is a book of memories.

There will be pictures of the child's birth mother and family, their early home, pets, first schooldays and later on, of course, letters from you. Each stage in the child's life is recorded, with the help of his or her social worker.

Clare's book

I saw Clare's book when she came to live with us as a foster child with a view to adoption. It had been started when she was first in care. It didn't make easy reading.

'The Life Story Book – which every child in care has and which they carry with them to each placement — is a record of their past and present, and it might help to shape their future.'

Depending on why a child was placed in care, pictures of their birth home might reveal a scene of disorder and confusion. Clare's home seemed to be a sea of piled-up bags, junk and clothes, with belongings strewn everywhere. This was a life of chaos and distress, with home merely a space to eat and sleep in, a discordant arena of desolation. But neglect was one of the reasons she was placed in care: and the reason most children are in care.

Some of the early pictures – when Clare and her siblings were first freed for adoption – showed a trio of children who were exceptionally thin and clearly malnourished, though smiling widely for the camera.

You may have to steel yourself for these impressions . . . for the child, these pictures are precious.

Child concern

'The books are normally cherished by the children who are in care – they are their main link with the past.'

The books are normally cherished by the children who are in care – they are their main link with the past. And, despite all the problems with their birth families, there is still love remaining, and often sorrow for the parents who treated them so badly.

You'd be surprised how caring small children can be to mothers who have neglected them, and this is as it should be. It shows that your foster child is capable of compassion. It means that despite all they've suffered, their feelings are not so badly bruised that they no longer feel any emotion at all.

Aide memoire

Children who grow up with the mother and father they were born to usually have plenty of opportunities to find out about their parents, their wider family members, the places they have lived in and their identities.

But children who experience separation from their birth families face obstacles when it comes to finding out about parents, grandparents and homes. There will very probably be gaps in the history that gives them their identity, the history that other children take for granted.

They might have to work out ways of dealing with difficult memories and emotions. They need to be able to explain what has happened to them and to move on to develop plans for the future.

Good things too

The Life Story Book can help a foster child to talk about loss, change and separation, and to remember the good things they've experienced, too. The Life Story Book is a positive project.

How to use it

At the start of my relationship with Clare, I found the Life Story Book almost overwhelming. Don't be alarmed if, like some foster parents, you'd almost be glad to throw it away!

But as the child moves on, more positive pictures will appear. These represent progress, fun with your family and new adventures for the child. Pictures of their life with you will also go into the book, and gradually it's an easier read.

Book benefits

One of the most vital benefits of Life Story work is that through it, your foster child can understand the reasons for their entry into out-of-home care and any later moves to new placements. He or she needs to piece together all of the fragments of their life.

Through the book, they will be able to make sense of their past and begin to get a balanced understanding of their present.

You won't see this at first, but you will as he or she matures into adulthood . . . gaining confidence may take longer than with children who were never in care.

Thanks at last

By the time she was 30, Clare was able to talk about her background; for years in her teens she never did.

'Through the book, they will be able to make sense of their past and begin to get a balanced understanding of their present.'

She even mentioned it, with surprising words of thanks to us, when she gave a little speech at a birthday party laid on for her in a local club by her friends. We were invited.

Cue then for a huge swig of bubbly before tears shot to my eyes . . . a few drinks now and again can be therapeutic when you foster!

The book goes too

Some foster children go back and forth between carers and birth family, and the book goes with them, bridging the gap between carers and parents. It's a visual record for when the child or young person returns home. Birth parents facing challenging times might feel they have missed out while their child was in care, and the Life Story Book can help them.

Life Story checklist:

Life Story Books can contain:

- Plastic sheets for copies of school reports, awards.
- Certificates etc.
- Memorabilia such as baby tags, ticket stubs, etc.

The child or young person may choose to include:

- Photos.
- A copy of his or her birth certificate.
- Drawings.
- Letters from their parents, friends, siblings or foster carers.
- Postcards and pictures of where they were born.
- Photos of past or current pets.
- Family tree.
- Holidays and special outings.

Foster parents can sit with their foster child from time to time and help them update their book. They can also take photographs of their foster child and ensure that schoolwork – drawings and writing the child is proud of – is included. Your foster child might have collections – stamps, stickers, celebrity pictures, pictures of pets or wildlife. They should go in the book, too.

Do:

- Let the child know that the book is confidential; that no one should see it without their permission.

- Help the child to keep the book in a safe place. Ask your foster child where he or she would like to store it.

- Ensure that the book goes with the child to new foster parents or adoptive parents.

Precious possessions

A child in care might also have a valued keepsake which was given to them by their mother when they were freed for adoption. Clare had a silver bracelet engraved with her name, which her mother gave her when she was placed in foster care.

The bracelet was a precious possession, as was a rag doll, a gift from Clare's last foster parents, who she loved. When she arrived to stay with them, she had no toys at all. The first thing her foster father did on the day she arrived was go out and buy her a doll. She cherished this gift.

Old toys best

Never be tempted to urge the child to transfer their affections to new gifts from you by pointing out how shiny and new they are. Everything in your house will be new to the child, so it's no wonder they cling to their familiar possessions.

You will be buying some new clothes for them, but also hang on to clothes they arrived with: these are familiar and offer a sense of reassurance.

'Everything in your house will be new to the child, so it's no wonder they cling to their familiar possessions.'

Soft toys they might bring with them might be well-worn and shabby, but to the child they are precious. These toys may have been with them since babyhood, and travelled with them in and out of care. Sometimes the toys offered the only comfort in a life of loneliness and sadness.

Keep adding

What you can do is be guided by your foster child on reading the Life Story Book and adding new pictures to it. No too many – work at his or her pace.

Summing Up

- Every foster child has a Life Story Book that he or she takes with them to every placement.

- The social worker begins the Life Story Book when the child first goes into care.

- The book might not make easy reading, but to your foster child it's a precious record.

- Help your child to maintain and add to her book.

- Children in care might have a keepsake gift from their birth mother.

Chapter Six

Contact With Birth Family

Meeting the family

One of your most challenging tasks as a foster parent could be meeting your child's birth family. There can be few foster parents who aren't anxious about this, and might even dread it. At the same time, you're bound to be curious, about his or her mother or father, and how the child reacts. You'll want to do your best in difficult circumstances.

Until the mid-80s, social workers used to speak of birth parents having 'access' to children in care; now the word used is 'contact'. All it means is that children are helped to maintain relationships with their birth family, and with other people from whom they've been separated. These could be previous foster carers, other foster children they have lived with (who could seem to them like brothers and sisters) and school friends.

Of course, the families from whom children have been removed might have neglected or deliberately harmed them. Yet contact might still be important. Everyone involved hopes for a good outcome, for the child to return to its birth home in safety and with the expectation of being properly looked after.

'One of your most challenging tasks as a foster parent could be meeting your child's birth family.'

Attachment

Contact meetings show children that their parents and other people they are attached to do not just disappear or forget them, even if they no longer take care of them. It sounds strange, yet to a child in care it makes sense.

Meetings help to maintain relationships, and they can also mend those that have been damaged. As circumstances change, so can relationships. They can improve and past hurts can be healed.

Not just good or bad

Contact can help children to remember their family as it really was. Separated children often visualise their parents in black and white terms – either all good or all bad. They may idealise them as perfect, or say they hate them. If they meet them, they might begin to form a more balanced view.

Contact boosts children's self-esteem and their sense of identity. They feel they are being taken seriously, that their life and their views are important.

Reassurance

Meeting the birth family reassures children that the people in their lives from whom they are separated are managing without them. Children in care can worry about their mothers, especially if they have been ill.

'Contact boosts children's self-esteem and their sense of identity.'

Foster children have often had to look after their siblings (Clare did) and protect them. They may have been left on their own all night. In foster care, the child who acted as 'mother' continues to worry about the siblings' welfare.

Not their fault

Meetings help preserve a child's memories and perhaps soften bad memories. Children need to know that separations are not their fault. They can have a tendency to blame themselves.

If children have a disability or a learning difficulty, they need to know that this was not the cause of the separation. They may feel that it was 'because of me' that they were 'not good enough' or did something wrong and are being punished.

Most importantly, contact reduces a child's feelings of loss, sadness and despair. It will not take away the pain of separation, but it leaves the door open for future possibilities.

Encourage contact

Encouraging and promoting contact is one of the most valuable things you can do as a foster parent. The child then knows they are loved and accepted just as they are, and that it's fine to see their families again.

Some foster carers see contact as a natural part of caring, while others find it disruptive and aren't convinced, anyway, that it helps the child, especially when the child has come from a background of neglect or harm. Of course, foster carers can get upset when they see a child they've begun to love distressed after a visit from their mother.

But if you can get over that, you are giving your foster child a great advantage.

Even very small children can keep absent mothers and other family members in mind for a long time, much longer than we as adults can imagine. Too many visits can be disturbing for everyone, yet too little contact can damage infant attachments.

'Encouraging and promoting contact is one of the most valuable things you can do as a foster parent.'

Visits can be reduced

If a child becomes distraught during or after a visit, and the mother, too, becomes distressed, it can become intolerable for the foster carer. It's fine to make this clear to your social worker, and to ask that visits be reduced. Your own morale is vital.

But remember that if a child doesn't seem to look forward to his or her mother's visits – or appears not to care when she leaves – then the attachment bonds are being damaged. The child begins to withdraw into a confused world of their own, where all attachments are elusive or unsafe.

There is a view that children must 'settle in' to a placement before they have any contact with their birth mother. But there's also an argument that says children settle more easily if there's continuity. Continuity is reassuring; prolonged separation can make foster children anxious.

What kind of contact?

There are different kinds of contact. Careful decisions are made on what's best for each child.

Children in long-term placements usually have less frequent contact than those who might be going home in the near future.

Most children in foster care have direct contact with birth family members, which usually means face-to-face meetings. These may be in the carer's home, or at a place chosen by the social worker.

Contact may not be easy to plan

If you find it uncomfortable or difficult to have the meeting at your own home, social workers will understand and will not insist. But sometimes the distances between the child and the birth family are too great to make face-to-face easy to organise.

Social workers might also change their assessment of the risk involved, or there could be other factors which make a face-to-face meeting unsuitable. If so, phone calls, letters or email can be used to keep the child directly in touch with their parents and other relatives. Carers don't normally see these letters or emails.

Letterbox contact

Sometimes it's necessary to keep the child's address confidential. In that case, letterbox or indirect contact is used. Letters, postcards, school reports, the child's drawings and any sort of communication are routed both ways through a third party, usually the child's social worker, and letters on both sides are generally checked before being sent on.

Use DVDs

DVDs and videos are a boon for keeping in touch. They're portable and can be looked at over and over again. They offer an active view of the child, and they can be a part of both direct and indirect contact.

Some foster carers make a video of the child at Christmas and on birthdays – the child can talk and tell his or her mum what they've been doing. Mothers can be filmed, too, and keep the child in care up to date with what's happening at home.

If there are new family members, the child can see and hear them. An advantage of a video is that a foster child can play it whenever they want, and on their own.

No contact at all?

Sometimes there is no contact. It might be that birth family members have died, or there could be legal reasons for a contact ban.

But do still try to help your foster child keep their birth family in mind, even if there's very limited contact or none at all. The child has a place in their heart for that birth family, and they have memories. If the mother has died, has a long-term illness or is in prison, the foster mother is doing a valuable service by keeping the mother's memory alive.

How?

Memories can be kept strong if you, as foster mother, keep an album for birth family photos and a box for special treasures. Your foster child might want to look at them with you from time to time.

Keep an up-to-date record of all the addresses which might be important to the foster child. For example, if their long-term social worker moves on, it's nice to keep contact details so that Christmas cards and news of the child's progress can be exchanged.

Making it work

It's time to help set up a meeting with birth family members, perhaps in your own home. You will definitely feel a bit anxious!

'Do still try to help your foster child keep their birth family in mind, even if there's very limited contact or none at all.'

Your social worker will support you, but make sure that contact arrangements with the birth family are in writing. Explain what will happen – a chat to keep in touch, and tea. Be clear about the date and the time. Tell them where your home is and how to get there. A rough sketch map always helps. Keep words as simple as possible in letters or emails.

If possible, the child should be involved in talking about the meeting first. Explain that it's not to rehash the situation, but just to have a catch-up and see each other. It's not to talk about the separation, or what happened in the past.

Progress catch-up

The contact meeting has begun. You can talk about the child's progress at school and any hobbies he or she has. The birth family might talk about pets or other children or friends of the child, or just what's new.

It's not so much what's said as how it's said.

It might be difficult, but as a foster parent you need to demonstrate respect and friendliness towards the birth mother, no matter how hard this might be. Children pick up quickly on tensions.

There is common ground

You might – or might not – find the birth family mother's personality and approach objectionable. Grit your teeth. When real family members have personalities and behaviours which are entirely different from yours, you might think you have nothing in common. Yet you do: you both care about the foster child.

Tensions can be eased by having things to do. Look at photos, or the child's work, so that the whole time isn't spent making conversation. During the meeting, it's good to have some activity – most people are not comfortable sitting in the same place and just talking for a couple of hours.

Going into the garden, showing off pets, serving refreshments will help to break up the time.

Disabled children have as much right to contact as other children. Foster parents have reported that disabled children cry and indicate their wish to see Mum or Gran. So if you are fostering a child with a disability, this is something to consider.

Getting on with them

Can you 'get on' with your foster child's birth family? Of course, it's strange meeting people you know might have neglected or harmed the child you are caring for. Sometimes birth families get confused about appointments or might not even turn up. That can be frustrating.

But if they were as resourceful and organised as you'd like, there would probably have been no need for their child to go into care. Keep this in mind when you feel frustrated by the birth mother's behaviour.

No confidence

Sometimes it might be that the birth mother lacks confidence, doesn't really know how to behave in social situations, or has never had a role model or anyone to teach her these things in the way good parents do. Being welcoming and friendly can make a huge difference.

You might find that a teenage foster child can also let you down by not keeping to an appointment. Once a child hits the teenage years – whatever their background – often it's their own friends who are of most importance to them. Seeing the birth family may be a chore to be avoided. You could find this disappointing and annoying.

By arrangement only

A birth parent or family member should never just turn up on your doorstep; it must be by arrangement. Your own family's privacy should never be invaded without warning.

If you have a good rapport with the birth family, it might be possible to arrange meetings without the social worker's input. Your experiences and views about each contact meeting will be taken into account – there will always be an opportunity to give feedback to social workers.

Sometimes the birth family might want to bring along other family members and friends to meetings. It might seem severe to limit the number of people at contact meetings, but you might have to. Check with the child's social worker about it. She will be on your side. If the meeting is to be at your home, you and you alone need to feel comfortable about the number of people who will be there.

Try tea

Birth families might feel intimidated if they feel your home is 'better' than theirs. Try to put them at ease. Offer tea, coffee and a small snack.

'Try not to see negative comments the birth mother might make as criticism of you.'

Child safety concerns?

Let the social worker worry about this – he or she is the person responsible for a foster child's safety during contact meetings, not the carer. They will take steps to avoid any threatening situations during contact. If contact is supervised by social workers for safety reasons, it's known as 'supported contact'.

But there might be occasions when a social worker asks you to supervise contact. You should stay in the room throughout the meeting. One of the dangers, if you are not there, is that the birth mother will tell the child that he or she will be going home soon, or that their father will come to collect them – promises (or lies) which will raise false expectations in the child's mind.

It's not criticism

Try not to see negative comments the birth mother might make as criticism of you. She might suggest changing the child's hairstyle or bring her different clothes.

It's easy to see this as criticism of the way you care for the child, but you can also see it as the mother increasing the attachment between her and the child.

Be prepared for some birth parents to say hurtful things about you. It can be a sign of their pain at having a child in care, or their shame at not having been good parents.

Quality not quantity

Don't forget that the quality of contact is more important than quantity. One good meeting at intervals is far better than many frequent meetings which end in tears.

Contact work

There is work to be done between contact meetings. You can talk to your child about the meeting in positive terms, try to praise the mother if she clearly has made an effort, and look forward to the next meeting.

The better the quality of contact, the better the outcome for the child in foster care.

Summing Up

- Most foster carers are nervous about meeting the child's birth mother.

- Contact reassures children that separation was not their fault.

- Contact might be by 'letterbox' only – post and email.

- DVDs are a boon for children and birth families.

- Give clear details about the day and time of the meeting, and how to find your home.

- Do your best to be welcoming and friendly to the birth mother . . . offer some refreshments if possible.

- Don't be upset if birth mothers seem to criticise you.

- Even if children are distressed afterwards, the meeting might still have helped them.

- Talk about the meeting to your foster child, and prepare positively for the next one.

Chapter Seven

Preparing a Child
for Adoption

One of the most valuable jobs that foster carers can take on is looking after children for whom adoption is planned. It is not easy or painless. It calls for strength and selflessness, and brings rewards.

If you are caring for a child destined for adoption, your social worker will support you and do the initial work of explaining to the child what will happen. It is likely that the child will have been in and out of care, and perhaps back to the birth home from time to time.

Social workers will have done everything possible to help the birth mother to keep the child, including arranging for a care worker to act as a 'home help' – going to the home several days to show the mother how to feed and look after her children – and setting up therapeutic support for her.

But if all the help ends in failure – as it often does – there will be a legal hearing to determine whether or not the child will be freed for adoption. At this time, the child will already be in foster care, probably in the same region in which he or she was born.

'One of the most valuable jobs that foster carers can take on is looking after children for whom adoption is planned. It is not easy or painless. It calls for strength and selflessness, and brings rewards.'

Forever family

Fostering is then an interim stage during which the child is gradually introduced to the idea of adoption – known as a 'forever family' – and eventually matched with prospective parents. It might be that the child to be adopted has been with you for some time, perhaps a year or more. If plans were initially for them to return home, these will have been changed. The child will have been through a lot.

Personal social worker

But remember that children are resilient, more so than adults. The child will have had a social worker that, ideally, she has known all the time she's been in care. This was the case with Clare when we met her. She had been fostered by the same family for two years, and there was much love and affection between them. They had seen this little girl through various changes of plan. They then had to negotiate her journey to being adopted by us: fostering first but with a view to adoption.

Helping the social worker to introduce the child to the idea of the 'forever family' isn't easy. The social worker will have told the child that she is doing her utmost to find the best possible family for them – and that the final choice is the child's.

'Helping the social worker to introduce the child to the idea of the "forever family" isn't easy.'

Exchange of letters

Letters and pictures will be exchanged, slowly but surely, and the potential adopters learn a lot about the child's background. But the two bits of the puzzle don't move at the same time and at the same speed. While the adoptive parents are waiting eagerly for news of their possible child, he or she may be with you, sad and anxious about their birth mother and still hoping that they'll be able to return home.

This is the main difficulty: events and emotions don't dovetail. You as foster carer will be the one who understands the child's fears and anxieties, and see how he or she might not be focused on adoption in the way the adoptive parents are.

Professional task

Preparing a child for permanence is a professional, demanding task. The average age at adoption is four years, but children may be younger or older. We fostered Clare, with a view to adoption, when she was eight years old. She had been in care for most of her life, and with her last foster parents – who she loved – for the past two years, all of which didn't make the transition simple for any of us.

Triangle of love

The foster carers grew very attached to Clare (and had applied unsuccessfully to adopt her), and we loved her instantly. It was a very difficult triangle, which was handled in an exemplary manner by social workers, foster carers and Clare – but not without some pain.

I was the one who handled it least well. Longing to adopt her (we had no other children) and enchanted by her personality, I was apt to see things only from my point of view. I'm older and wiser now – I see only too clearly how much the foster parents had done, what skill and love they'd shown, only to have to give her to us.

Can you be stoic?

So, this is a part of the job that takes most out of foster carers. You need heaps of understanding, the strength to accept decisions you might not like, and the stoicism needed to cope with the loss of a dear child.

High price – but with a bonus

'Foster carers who help children to move on to adoption can pay a high emotional price,' says Bath social worker, Sarah Acheson. 'Foster carers will vary in how difficult they find this and whether it is something they can keep doing – but some do it over and over for years or even decades.'

The reward for the carers can be a complex and crucial job well done; a child's life made better by being given the skilled early help they need.

In a really good transition from fostering to adoption, the foster carer and adopters will develop a very positive relationship which endures for the long-term benefit of the child. This is an achievement you can always be proud of.

'You need heaps of understanding, the strength to accept decisions you might not like, and the stoicism needed to cope with the loss of a dear child.'

Questions, questions

Children being placed with new permanent families are often contending with moves from poorly-understood pasts to what may be very different but equally unknown futures. As they move to an adoptive family, they are likely to experience a range of intense, perhaps conflicting, emotions.

Their early years in foster placements may have had a profound impact on how they regard family life. They are bound to have many questions: How safe will the new family be? What does love and care mean in this family? How can I best survive there? What will happen to the people in my first family? Will I ever see them again? How will my foster mum cope without me? What will these new people think of me?

Take it step by step . . .

Let's look at the steps you take to prepare a foster child for permanence:

'Talk about what a new family might be like.'

1 – The child is first placed with you, foster carer:

- Create a relationship with the child within which questions can be asked and feelings explored openly.
- Collect objects (from birth family, hospital, your family, school, nursery, outings) for the child's memory box.
- Start taking photos.
- Listen to birth family members if possible.
- Help the child start a diary for memories.

2 – Assessment and planning

- Keep alive the idea that children don't stay with you forever (with play, talking, books).
- Talk about what a new family might be like.

- Keep recording your family life.

- Contribute to the Life Story Book work.

- Link in with the child and your own social worker to share ideas and avoid duplication – clarify what each is doing.

- Acknowledge your own feelings about moving on, and support the child in theirs.

3 – Adoptive family identified!

- Share the adopters' book about themselves with the child – the social worker will give this to you.

- Increase play/books/talking about the move.

- Plan for goodbyes with school, nursery, extended family etc.

- Ask for all the information you need about timescales/expectations.

4 – You meet the adopters

It's time for you to meet the adopters, probably at their home. It'll be just you, them and the social worker. The child will not be there. The adoptive parents will want to know about the child's routine, their likes and dislikes, typical ups and downs.

5 – Everyone meets

The day arrives when you're all to meet the would-be adoptive parents for the first time. Nerves all round! Expect the foster child to be overexcited and nervous, perhaps asking you to even postpone the meeting.

The child's social worker will shoulder most of the burden, but you as a foster carer have a huge part to play. The more positive you are about adoption – and the more you can calm the child's fears – the better things will go.

Children pick up quickly on adults' hidden faces. If you have doubts about whether the child should be adopted, or whether the selected adopters are right for them, your anxieties can be conveyed without you saying a single word.

Make them welcome!

As the prospective adopters arrive, don't be surprised if the foster child dodges away or hides in their room. Clare did run down to the car to see us, smiled, and then ran off. She admitted she was nervous – but she did come back again after a short while.

It's likely that this first meeting will be centred on a meal of some kind, most probably tea at your home. Your child's social worker will be there too.

Ice breakers

Of course, this isn't any ordinary tea party. There is ice – quite a lot of it – to be broken; it can feel a little unreal. You will probably feel very strange to be sitting with new people who will be your child's parents – especially if she already calls you Mummy. Foster children are encouraged to treat foster parents as their mum and dad. The relationship with foster parents is delicate, and especially so when their attachment to the child is obvious.

Small talk

At this first tea, you might talk about general subjects – what's in the news, local gossip – as adults do. Talking to the child all the time will put a strain on him or her.

Clare's foster parents encouraged her to show us her room and spend a little time with us in the garden on her own. This was good of them, and much appreciated.

'It's not just the adopters who need to be happy with the match – the child does too, and so do you as foster carers.'

Mention forever

Potential adopters might try to avoid mentioning the word 'adoption' to the child. We didn't say it; I thought it would frighten her. After all, she had a choice as well. But when the social worker saw us afterwards to debrief us on the meeting, we were told that Clare was upset because we never mentioned it. She thought we didn't like her.

It's not just the adopters who need to be happy with the match – the child does too, and so do you as foster carers. Don't mention any misgivings you might have to the parents, but do raise them with social workers. Your thoughts will be asked for.

Because we hadn't been demonstrative enough to Clare, that first meeting was assessed as slightly unsatisfactory by the social worker and foster family. As the foster carer, you'll know the child well; he or she might have been with you for several years, so you more than anyone can decode the child's reaction and get an idea of what they are really feeling. Even small children can be good at putting on a show, saying or doing what they think is expected of them.

Good gifts?

Adoptive parents might want to give presents of clothes to the child, which might differ from the clothes you've bought. Mums invest a lot in what their kids wear, and it doesn't feel good when you see choices which are quite different from yours.

Bear with the adoptive parents. We bought Clare clothes and toys we liked. I suppose I subconsciously wanted her to fit in with our 'idea' of her. But times are changing rapidly for the child in care – he or she wants to stick with familiar things, like the clothes they've been used to wearing when they're with you, the foster carers, and the toys they had then.

'As the foster carer, you'll know the child well; so you more than anyone can decode the child's reaction and get an idea of what they are really feeling.'

6 – Bad behaviour follows good

The child spends a day, then a weekend, then a week with her adoptive family. Help them make little lists of what to take and what to bring back. This is an exciting yet nervous time for them – they will relax when they're back with you, but also might behave badly, too.

They'll exploit it!

They'll know they are the apple of the adoptive parents' eye, and will very probably exploit it! They might also bring back gifts they were given and show off a bit. Put up with it – it's a natural reaction. Let them talk, and show them you're pleased they had a good time – be positive.

7 – Goodbye!

This is when you say a final farewell. You have the tough job of helping to pack the child's belongings, loading the car, and then the final embrace. It's not easy for you.

Don't be surprised if the child cries or tries to hang on to you – that's all to be expected. Give the child a little gift to be opened later. Clare's foster parents were most generous, giving her a new CD player.

Long journey

The adoptive parents will be accompanied by the child's social worker, who will remain with them on the journey. My memory of Clare is that she cried for a good part of the journey home, but as we drew into Bath – her new city – she perked up a bit. It was enormously helpful that her social worker was sitting next to her all the way.

You deserve a treat

Foster carers should arrange a small treat for themselves that evening – a movie, a meal with friends – while also acknowledging their feelings and accepting that they might feel down. Again, you'll get support from your own social worker – lots. But you, foster carer, of all people need pampering on this day.

What next?

After the placement you can agree expectations about future contact, be available for visits from the child and adopters, post items the child left behind, and send cards and photographs to the child. Staying in touch is vital.

You helped first and most

When an adoption has been carried out positively, the long-term rewards are significant. The child can flourish and progress to a future with every possible advantage. But it's you, the foster carer, who put him or her on the road to success and laid the foundations for their happiness.

'It's you, the foster carer, who put him or her on the road to success and laid the foundations for their happiness.'

Summing Up

- Children are resilient – they can cope with changing homes, and new parents.

- Foster children can still be very nervous when they first meet possible adopters.

- Calm their fears and make the first meeting with new parents positive.

- Bear with adoptive parents if they give too many gifts at the start.

- When your foster child leaves for their new life, expect some tears.

- Factor in a treat for you that evening – you deserve it.

- Stay in touch with your foster child and new family!

- Remember – you did all the hardest groundwork.

- Your foster child will always remember you – don't doubt it.

Chapter Eight

Fostering Difficult Children

Would you like to care for children who will be more difficult to look after – children who have come from very bad backgrounds? Fostering these more testing children means taking the love with the hate. On the receiving end of resentment and anger, you will be taking on a challenging assignment.

Young offenders

There are foster schemes specifically for young people on the edge of, or already involved in, offending. Some may have already been involved in petty crime – theft, perhaps, or vandalism. The thing to remember is they all have suffered distressing childhoods – their behaviour didn't come out of the blue.

These young people can be fostered and mentored at the same time – foster carers who are able to chat with them about future plans and help them on the road to success are very much sought after. You don't have to be part of a couple to foster these children – you could be a single mum or dad with grown children, for example. Although it's a hard job, it can also be an interesting one.

Good money

Fees can be good; as much as between £322 and £574 a week per child, plus a variety of allowances and training. There is 24-hour support and respite care when you need it . . . which you probably will from time to time.

'Fostering more testing children means taking the love with the hate. On the receiving end of resentment and anger, you will be taking on a challenging assignment.'

Antisocial children

You will want your foster child to fit into your routine, but there will be children who seem antisocial. They might seem sullen and withdrawn, not wanting to play or take part in family activities. In a word, they will seem unpleasant – or 'challenging'.

You would be paid more for looking after a child like this, but you would be giving a lot more.

How would you handle a child who is such hard work?

Don't force it

'You would be paid more for looking after a child like this, but you would be giving a lot more.'

One foster mother told me that it's never a good idea to try to force the child to join in with the foster family:

'Let them stay in their room, be alone, look at their own toys or possessions – or even just be unhappy. The worst thing you can do is try to make it better, telling the child to buck up or pull themselves together. The best plan is always to give them a choice . . . say, "We're watching a DVD tonight . . . you're very welcome to join us if you'd like to." Always emphasise that you would love it if they wanted to join you – but equally it's fine if they choose not to.'

No choice

The one area where there isn't a choice is meals. If your family routine is tea after school at 5.30pm every day, then this isn't an option. Children, in care or not, must eat regularly and properly. You shouldn't have the burden of cooking separate meals, either. It's one thing if a child has an allergy, but if they just 'prefer' pizza and won't eat anything else, then they'll just have to think again.

'I do try to serve meals I know kids will enjoy, but I also like them to taste new things from time to time,' says Carey Meredith, an experienced foster parent near Bristol. 'And, certainly, they wouldn't be allowed to have a sweet if they hadn't eaten the main course.'

Boundaries

Patience and firmness are the two keys to looking after children whose behaviour is difficult.

'You need to set boundaries,' says one foster mother. 'And you need to expect difficult behaviour. You will be less stressed if you accept that there will be challenges. It's part of the job. If they behaved well and had had a good upbringing, would they be in care? It's pointless to judge them by conventional standards.'

Boundary checklist

Boundaries can include:

- Not going into the parents' bedroom or other children's bedrooms unless invited.
- Watching TV and using the computer at agreed times for the agreed number of hours.
- No smoking and drinking, and no drugs in the house.
- Always let foster parents know where they are – and staying overnight only with friends whose family you've met, or on school trips.
- Eating with the family – not making their own separate meals in your kitchen.
- Invite friends over only by arrangement.
- Keep to a set bedtime.
- Keep his/her room reasonably tidy.
- Put clothes for washing in a laundry basket.

'Patience and firmness are the two keys to looking after children whose behaviour is difficult.'

Walk away

If they try to argue with you, are rude or insult you, you must ignore it and walk away. Once you start to respond, you have come down to a child's level and the argument will just accelerate.

I've done it myself; I said things I wished I hadn't, and it's exhausting.

If you walk away and refuse to respond to rudeness, they will calm down after a while – it's inevitable. And once that happens, don't bear a grudge.

Consequences

Carey Meredith says the best way to deal with difficult behaviour is to always make children aware of the consequences of their actions.

Rather than punish them, make them see that what they have said or done has led to a situation that they then will regret.

Live with it

'For example, I had a child who trashed his bedroom – scrawling on the wallpaper, ripping up curtains and ruining the room. We could have had it redecorated; that sort of expense is met by the fostering agency. But instead, we delayed redecoration for some time, enough for him to realise the consequences of his actions. While the room was in a state, no friends were allowed in to visit, as the room was such a mess.

'So he had to live with this room for a while, and live with not having friends in. I can't remember how long it was – certainly a few weeks – before we did redo the room, but his behaviour was never as bad again. He realised that the state of the room was his decision and his alone. To live in a nice room again meant he had to tone down his behaviour – then he was able to match up action with consequence. Once a child begins to do that, you have made a difference.'

Create conscience

When children can match up actions to consequences, they also begin to develop a conscience about what they have done. They see the results of their bad behaviour. They start to regret it. The message might go in: it's best not to act that way again, or the same thing will happen.

Withhold treats

Carey also punished bad behaviour by withholding treats: favourite TV programmes, going out with friends or having them round.

No smacks

That urge to smack or say sharp words – which all parents have now and again – has to be strenuously controlled. Smacking a child or using threatening behaviour or words is not an option for foster parents – it's banned – so discipline has to be more carefully thought out. You get good training and support.

No threats

The foster child must never threaten your own child's safety. Here you need common sense. All kids quarrel from time to time, and what seems like a violent argument between them could just replicate a normal brother-sister fight.

It isn't for everyone

Not all foster carers can cope with disturbed children. One foster carer decided to take on difficult short-term children who were on the fringes of law-breaking – petty stealing, staying out all night and running away.

After several months of assessment and training, she was matched with her first challenging children, but after a year found it too much. Two children stole from her and two ran away, brought back by police in the early hours of the morning, with the incidents waking her neighbours.

'Smacking a child or using threatening behaviour or words is not an option for foster parents – it's banned – so discipline has to be more carefully thought out. You get good training and support.'

Broken nights

Yet she still tried hard, sitting down with them and talking through their future plans, offering advice from her own experience as a mum. One girl liked her so much she asked to be placed with her again. But by then the broken nights, the anxiety over missing children and the bad behaviour had taken its toll; she reluctantly decided the job was not for her.

Blame

'There was some threatening behaviour,' she recalls. 'I had to lock away all alcohol and sharp knives. When children were brought back by the police in the early hours, police would blame me for letting the children out, but as a foster parent, you are not allowed to keep teenagers in under lock and key, they have to have some freedom.

'I would have liked to continue; I wanted to help and thought some children had real potential. But I just didn't have the energy to put up with constant trouble and disruption to my own life.'

Too high a price

This carer admits that the fee was good – when she had two children, £800 plus a week. 'To me that was extremely good money. Of course it wasn't every single week as it was short-term care. There are allowances on top of that. Yet when I took everything into account, the cost of earning that amount of money was too high for me.'

Social workers will never judge you if you find you can't manage this kind of foster care; you can still be considered for other types of fostering. Your work will still be much appreciated. Don't feel bad about it – they understand.

Energy boost

A challenging child can hit your energy levels. When this happens, professional counselling can be a great help – and it's free if the child is being helped by CAMHS, the Child and Adolescent Mental Health Service. CAMHS will also be supportive for the carers.

Using CAMHS counselling – both face-to-face and online – carers can develop a deeper understanding of the child's needs and also the impact on themselves as foster parents. They can begin to understand the child's behaviours and can learn effective strategies to deal with them. Carers can also seek counselling through their GP, and the social worker is there too, to support you.

You do need people to talk to – people who understand the work. You'll find that some friends and relatives are often useless at being helpful – they fail to understand why you do the job.

Same time counselling

One foster carer I spoke to found the CAMHS therapy very useful. She has her counselling at the same time as the 16-year-old girl she is looking after.

'I can drive us both, so it takes only one journey,' she says. 'Therapy is very useful – you can talk over any problems you're experiencing with your child, and also about your own feelings. I always feel more relaxed after I've had my counselling, and I seem to sleep better. We go once a month. And of course it's all free. I look on it as a bonus of the job, really. It's definitely worth having.'

Respite care for you

If a child is constantly difficult, respite care is available – when the child goes to other carers for a weekend. This gives you a chance to get your breath back and have some time to yourself. Where children are in long-term care they may get to know their regular respite carers well, so that visiting them carries little stress. Regular respite care can work well.

'If a child is constantly difficult, respite care is available – when the child goes to other carers for a weekend.'

Contact with birth family

This might be an area which sparks off bad behaviour, especially if children already have difficult personalities. One of the most common criticisms of contact in foster care is that children and their birth families do not seem to relate to each other in a normal, positive way.

This is why some foster parents dread contact meetings, because they know what the fallout will be like later on.

Contact might reawaken trauma for children if they see a person who has abused or failed to protect them in the past. It's you as foster carer who will be able to detect signs of stress in your foster child. Foster carers are in the best position to monitor impact of contact on the children they look after. If there are doubts and misgivings, regular discussions and reviews with the child's social worker can lead to improved arrangements.

Child's wish comes first

However, almost all children are attached to their parents, no matter how badly they have been treated. If the child wishes to continue contact, this wish is respected. Contact – despite the potential for problems – might offer the opportunity to mend relationships.

Monitor certain contact

Teenagers who make the arrangements for contact themselves might also be monitored if contact could put them at risk. There might be situations in which brothers and sisters have been forced to participate in sexual acts together – or siblings may have a history of mistreating one another.

Contact then needs to be supported. In any case, you as foster carer need clear details about your role in the contact arena. Is it just to deliver and collect the child for meetings, or to be there during contact to help the child feel more confident? Get your social worker to make this crystal clear.

Signed agreement

Foster carers should have their own signed agreement for each placement . . . so make sure you have this and keep it in a safe place. Read it carefully. Some foster carers have reported having the foster child's mother just turn up at their homes without warning, when this was not in the agreement.

Hang on to patience

Others have reported children becoming distraught during and after visits from their birth mum because they sense the imminent partings. Their prolonged distress can alarm the foster carer, and disrupt the household.

All and any of these situations can provoke bad behaviour. Again, you need that mix of patience, compassion and strength: and to keep talking to your social worker. If visits become too stressful, social workers might look at other options for the child – perhaps to reduce visits.

Talents, too!

It's not all bad. You'd be surprised how children who are sometimes difficult show a talent for writing, since they spend a lot of time in their own imagination, and they have unconventional material to mine. Or, their talent may be for drawing and art, or music or acting.

When Clare was nine, the children in her class were asked to draw something that most reminded them of home. Most of the children drew teddy bears, cakes or their mum's smiling face. Clare drew my husband David's tie in black and white, knotted loosely, where he'd left it before going away on a trip. It somehow summed up both her love for him and the fact that he was often away on business. The tie was there, almost as though around his neck, but he was not. It seemed to hold the memory of him.

Creative children

Teachers praised this very careful drawing, both for its detail and originality – the tie seemed to 'speak'. It's framed now. That's just one example; I know of plenty more where foster children showed unusual creativity, perhaps stimulated by their background.

One foster boy, who had displayed difficult behaviour, became a successful local club DJ when he was 18 – his confidence, freed by sensitive foster carers who never gave up on him, also released his talent for music. There are more success stories in the final section of this book!

They've healed, thanks to you

Foster children might have strange and disturbing material to draw on, as well as their turbulent journey through care. They've endured so much more than children who had loving birth families and stable homes. But thanks to you, the foster carer, they have healed so much as well.

'Foster children might have strange and disturbing material to draw on, as well as their turbulent journey through care. But thanks to you, the foster carer, they have healed so much as well.'

Summing Up

- Set firm boundaries when foster children join your home.

- Allow them solitude when they want it.

- Mealtimes are not optional.

- High fees are paid for fostering/mentoring children who are young offenders, or on the edge of offending.

- Respite care for foster children is available to give you a regular break.

- There may be useful private counselling for you if your foster child is in the CAMHS service (Child and Adolescent Mental Health Service).

- Contact with birth family may lead to bad behaviour.

- Some contact may need to be monitored.

- Foster parents need a signed agreement for each placement – read carefully.

- Foster children can be creative too – with special allowances to pay for extra classes.

Chapter Nine

Final Words: Moving On

You're now a foster parent and, I hope, enjoying the job, despite its ups and downs. Helping the child move on is the final challenge. At 16 or 17, a local authority must provide accommodation to a child in need. This could be 'supported lodgings', a small group home with a helper, a Housing Association flat or help finding college accommodation.

Whatever the next move, if the child has been with you a while, he or she will be leaving home with all of the anxieties that this will bring.

Survival skills

How do young people who have grown up in care survive without a safety net to fall back on? How do they get through the turmoil of the late teens and early 20s without the emotional and financial support of a loving family behind them? In other words, how do these young people make it?

Many do, but there are many who don't. Some years ago, a government minister wrote to local authority councillors and officials asking them to do for care leavers just what they would do for their own children. That message remains as relevant today as it was then. Many care leavers tell of being ill–equipped to suddenly cope on their own.

Success stories

There are great success stories, too. The Adolescent and Children's Trust (TACT www.tactcare.org.uk) – is the country's largest charity provider of fostering and adoption services.

'Helping the child move on is the final challenge.'

It launched a course for young people over 16 who are in care to help them move into an independent life. Units covered health, social skills, moving on, jobs, money matters and managing your home. Already four foster children have completed the course.

Self-development awards

Awards for personal improvement and self-development went to a 16-year-old who completed the Three Peaks Challenge, climbing the three highest peaks in the UK, and a 19-year-old living in supported lodgings passed her driving test, a huge achievement for her.

High grades

'Believe in and expect the best for every young person you work with and support them to achieve it.'

Other success stories include a foster girl who sat her GCSE exams early and achieved the highest grades in maths and chemistry, and a six-year-old who won a prize for scoring well above average marks in literacy, and a 13-year-old boy who had a poor school attendance record and a smoking habit before being placed in foster care . . . now he now has 100 percent attendance at school and he's quit smoking.

Awards for carers too

TACT recognises the work of foster carers, too. One dedicated carer who won an award was looking after a child who refused to speak – she was a selective mute. Yet thanks to the carer's support, that child now talks again . . . a marvellous tribute to the carer.

That's just one example of the many inspirational success stories of the ways vulnerable foster children are helped to move into maturity. Other foster agencies arrange awards and presentations for carers and children – achievements by both are celebrated today.

The message is – believe in and expect the best for every young person you work with and support them to achieve it.

Money matters!

The area where they might need the most help is managing money, and that's easier said than done. Clare took on the practical skills with ease; she passed her driving test at 17, and did her own laundry from the age of 12.

No cash

But handling money was a different matter. She never saved any. She would lend friends money and never get it back. She took on part-time selling work with companies such as Avon, then allowed friends 'credit' while she paid the costs for them . . . which they didn't reimburse.

She would let some repay her with Boots and WH Smith gift vouchers which she spent while meeting their bills in cash! She ran up large debts by spending colossal amounts on barely-worn shoes and clothes. She needed bail outs and debt counselling.

Trad – not tech – life skills

Here are some practical, tried and tested life tools you can instil to help a young person be safe and independent. Don't rely too much on high technology here. Kids are addicted to it, but when there's a panic, it's the very basic knowledge they need.

- As soon as they are old enough, go to the local train and bus stations with them and show them how a rail timetable works. Despite the Internet age, many young people still haven't a clue how to deal with public transport timetables.

- When catching trains and buses to new places, children should check and double check that they're on the right train or bus. Check with a rail or bus worker, and not a passenger, who might also be on the wrong train!

- Explain how to make a transfer charge call from a public phone box – should they ever be stranded and stuck without a mobile.

- Suggest keeping a £20 note 'untouchable' in their wallet, to be used only in an emergency – to get a taxi for example.

- They should always have a note of your address and phone numbers with them, so you could be traced if there's an accident . . . and they can call you.

- Encourage them to have driving lessons – as expensive as they can be these days – as soon as they can. It's worth giving them as a birthday present, as boring as they might sound! But getting family and friends to teach them is the road to driving test failure.

- If really in trouble – lost money, can't get home, phone not working – a young person can always go into the nearest police station and ask for help. My experience of police officers is that they are very helpful if you're on your own and in an unsafe situation or stranded.

- When a young person needs somewhere to sit safely while waiting to be collected, a museum or art gallery is free, has seats and loos and often coffee.

- Advise them against lending large sums of money to friends; children who have been in care can be too trusting for their own good.

- Remind them to wear bags across the shoulder, keep them fastened, never put them on the ground and leave them, even for a minute. Even apparently sensible adults I have known made this silly mistake – to their heavy cost.

- When travelling, they ought to write out a proper itinerary, with contact details and flight times and numbers – as much info as possible. Tell them to keep this in their bag, in an outside zipped pocket.

- If they're flying, persuade them to take only carry-on hand luggage, which goes with them in the cabin. Tracing a lost suitcase abroad – and they do go missing! – could be the last straw for a young person with limited confidence. They can pack a lot into carry-on cases – show them how.

- Are they staying in a hostel or hotel? Remind them to take a card from the lobby which has its name, address and phone number on. If they get lost, they know the address to get back to, by cab or on foot. I can't count the number of lost young people in Bath who have asked *me* where they are staying! 'Somewhere near the river . . . do you know it?'

'Don't say goodbye forever! Keeping in contact with a child who has been in your care will be of huge value to them.'

86

※ Get them to invest in street maps. They're the best way to find places they haven't been to before.

Stay in touch!

Don't say goodbye forever! Keeping in contact with a child who has been in your care will be of huge value to them. Send birthday cards and Christmas gifts. Visit them. Encourage the child to keep you updated with mobile numbers and email addresses. Depending on how close you and the child have become, tell them they can ring you if they feel low.

When you've worked with young people who are preparing to leave care and step into life as independent young adults, you give them the gift of a future. You can't put a price on the reassurance they will feel when they know there's someone who is 'family' in their life.

You've given them so much, so generously – and seeing them succeed will be the reward you never hoped for! It's a professional job that's really worth doing. As a foster carer, you'll always be one of a group of exceptional people.

'You've given them so much, so generously – and seeing them succeed will be the reward you never hoped for!'

Chapter Ten

FAQs

Can anyone foster?

Fostering is open to anyone - married, single, same-sex couples. A criminal record does not bar you from fostering, but you are not permitted to foster children if you, your partner or any member of your household has been cautioned or convicted for any sexual or violent offence against a child.

Am I too old?

Foster carers need to be over 18 (21 for some agencies) in England and Wales. There's no upper age limit, but you need enough energy and stamina to cope. A health report from your GP is part of the assessment process.

Must I be married?

No. Unmarried couples, singles, divorcees and those in a same-sex relationship are allowed to foster.

Will I be an employee of the foster agency?

All foster carers are self-employed. Your fees are paid direct into your bank or building account. There is tax relief for foster carers.

Is it a full-time job?

Certain children in care – maybe disabled or with special needs – will be a full-time job, but children at school enable the foster carer free time during the day, which you can use in any way. Foster caring requires a high level of commitment and is increasingly viewed as a profession in itself. There are some meetings and short training courses to attend.

How do I get accepted to be a foster carer?

There are no qualifications, but there is a formal assessment process – social workers meet you at your home – and training, plus police and health checks, and you'll need two referees. Agencies are looking for a positive personality and the ability to commit to a child. Once you pass your assessment, you are then approved for a particular child. You don't have to pass any exams or tests.

Can I choose what sort of placements I want?

There is a careful matching process, and all placement referrals are discussed with you. You only accept placements that you are comfortable with, and which feel right for your family.

What if things go wrong?

You are not expected to cope alone – often there is a 24-hour emergency helpline, and a social worker will be on your side to help you through problems. As foster carer, you are part of a team with extensive support.

Must I be well off?

Adoption agencies need to see that you can support yourself and your family, but you don't need to be affluent.

Do I need to own my home?

No – you can be a home owner, council tenant or private tenant – all acceptable.

I am a smoker/very overweight. Will this affect whether I can foster?

There are no blanket bans on who can foster, in terms of physique or health. But your health and lifestyle is taken into account, as are the risks of passive smoking.

What is the difference between an independent foster agency and the local authority?

Independent agencies (IFAs) work in partnership with the local authority. They provide foster care placements that, for one reason or another, the local authority have not been able to offer. These IFA placements may include more challenging children, disabled children, or children with special needs. The assessment, training and approval process is more or less the same: all agencies are in competition for the best foster parents.

I have my own children already. Can I still foster?

Yes. Your own children can be an asset in welcoming the foster child. But people without children are also welcomed by foster agencies.

Do foster children ever return to their birth parents?

The majority of children in the care system have been removed from birth parents for different reasons – usually for their own safety. All foster children have a care plan drawn up for them by their agency, and this may include returning to their birth family, and contact with them while in foster care.

Do I meet the foster child's birth parents?

Where there is contact between foster child and birth family, it will be part of your job to help the child prepare for contact meetings, to reassure them and perhaps host the meeting at your home. Social workers provide you with excellent support, and will usually be there at the contact meetings.

If a foster child is to be adopted, do I help with that?

Your help in preparing a child for adoption is invaluable. As with all aspects of the job, you get good training. You can choose whether you wish to have foster children who may be adopted placed with you – or if you prefer long-term fostering only – or emergency fostering. There are a variety of job options, with good training for each one.

Are there enough fostering jobs available?

There are far more children in care than foster parents to give them a home – there's absolutely no shortage of work.

Where do I start looking?

You can look on the Internet – there are many agencies seeking foster carers – or contact your local authority fostering team (look in the Yellow Pages). Local magazines and newspapers often carry advertisements for foster carers. The help list section of this book carries details of websites which will assist. An information welcome pack will get you started – then you make your application. After that, assessment, then approval – and your first placement. The entire process is friendly and welcoming. Your work is very much needed.

Help List

Awards, information, services

www.tactcare.org.uk
Adolescent and Children's Trust – UK's largest charity provider of fostering and adoption services. Runs Skills 4 Life courses for over-16s who are in care, plus a number of achievement awards for carers and foster children.

BAAF (British Association of Adoption & Fostering)

www.baaf.org.uk
First port of call for would-be foster parents – huge range of resources, all you need to know. Start here on your fostering journey!

CAMHS (Child and Adolescent Mental health Services)

www.camhscares.nhs/uk
Very positive NHS site with information on services provided for children, and foster families working in the mental health arena. Children with behavioural difficulties and their carers can benefit. A lively site which also includes tips and exercises on relaxation, sleep, positive living, coping with depression and more.

Choosing an agency

www.simplyfostering.co.uk

An organisation which helps you find the best fostering agency for you. Government advice is that you look at what several agencies have to offer before you make your decision. This useful site gives clear advice on fees offered by a choice of agencies.

Courses

www.open.ac.uk

The Open University offers a good range of social care courses, useful for foster carers working with small children – no qualifications are needed. You can download a prospectus or call 0845 300 60 90. Bursaries and fee reductions available.

The Fostering Network

www.fostering.net
Confidential advice line for foster carers and potential carers.

Pensions

www.pensionservice.gov.uk
As a foster carer, your years of working at home count towards your state pension and it is protected – you won't lose out. More details from this site.

Training and financial support for foster parents

www.directgov.uk/adoptionfostering
Information on training schemes and finance foster parents are entitled to.

Book List

Attachment, Trauma and Resilience
By Kate Cairns, BAAF, London, 2006.
Social worker Kate Cairns and her husband fostered 12 children over 25 years – all are still part of her family group. Her story helps foster carers to respond to traumatised children and help them with everyday situations. There is generous advice for foster parents on how to promote recovery and develop resilience in foster children who have been emotionally damaged.

Children's Special Needs
BAAF, London 2010.
All the information about extra needs many foster children will have – this is a leaflet, costing £1 from BAAF.

Foster Care and Social Networking
By Eileen Fursland, BAAF, London 2001.
Social networking throws up headaches faced by all involved with fostering. This book shows foster parents and children how to make the most of social networking opportunities, minimise online risks, and protect privacy and security.

Managing Difficult Behaviour
By Clare Pallett, Kathy Blackeby, William Yule, Roger Weissman, Stephen Scott and Eileen Fursland, BAAF, London 2008.
Advice on developing a better relationship with your foster child – with tips, case examples, exercises to help improve and ease your life together.

Preparation and Assessment Process (Fostering)
BAAF, London 2010.
This is aimed at foster carers who have already been accepted by an agency, and are now starting assessment and preparation course. A leaflet, costing £1, from BAAF.

Understanding Looked After Children: An introduction to psychology for foster carers
By Jeune Guishard-Pine, Suzanne McCall and Lloyd Hamilton: foreword by Andrew Wiener.
Jessica Kingsley Publishers, London, 2007.
Hugely helpful resource for first-time foster carers or experienced foster parents. The authors have had years of experience working with foster carers and foster children: they offer practical advice which de-mystifies the process of care, and gives insights into the children who are fostered.

  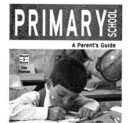  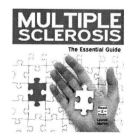